BERGERAC

NOTES

including
- *Introduction and Life of Rostand*
- *List of Characters*
- *Synopsis of the Play*
- *Summaries and Commentaries*
- *Character Analyses and Critical Commentaries*
- *Review Questions and Essay Topics*
- *Bibliography*

by
Estelle and LaRocque DuBose
Department of Languages and Literature
Western State College of Colorado

LINCOLN, NEBRASKA 68501

Editor	Consulting Editor
Gary Carey, M.A. *University of Colorado*	*James L. Roberts, Ph.D.* *Department of English* *University of Nebraska*

ISBN 0-8220-0346-5
© Copyright 1971
by
C. K. Hillegass
All Rights Reserved
Printed in U.S.A.

1994 Printing

Cliffs Notes, Inc.   Lincoln, Nebraska

CONTENTS

Cyrano de Bergerac Notes

INTRODUCTION

The classical tradition of French drama was formalized in the seventeenth century, and the eighteenth century was an imitation of the seventeenth. During this time, the plays were usually centered around characters from history—most often Greek or Roman history or literature—and were of a psychological nature. Any action which was violent or shocking, such as a battle, was simply told about and never re-enacted on stage. Aristotle's unities were closely observed—that is, the action took place within a time span of no more than 24 hours, in one geographical location, and concerned one main character.

The state of French drama during the nineteenth century was as tumultuous as was the state of French politics. Victor Hugo broke the restrictive chains of French classicism with the famous "Preface" to *Cromwell* (1827), the manifesto of romanticism. Over the next 25 years his dramas employed action as well as other dramatic devices denied to the classicists. During this period of literary and political upheaval, the schools of romanticism, naturalism, symbolism, and realism developed in France. Yet *Cyrano de Bergerac* does not really fit into any of these categories. Some have considered it a revival or culmination of romantic drama, but it did not truly revive this school nor continue it. *Cyrano* was presented in 1897 for the first time, half a century after Hugo's last effort, and is not a part of any school or movement.

Rather, *Cyrano* seems an outgrowth of the medieval French literature—the songs of the troubadours. Most notable of these were the *Chanson de Roland* and *Roman de la Rose*. The tales of Roland concerned a hero, brave, noble, loyal, and steadfast, who avenges any affront by killing the offender, and whose word is his bond. The *Roman de la Rose* is the prime example of the other kind of popular literature of that period, the type which idealized Woman and Love. The love in these tales was respectful, submissive, almost religious. *Cyrano* combines these two genres in its central character and its story. Rostand himself came from southern France where these tales originally developed and where the historical Cyrano de Bergerac had his roots.

Cyrano can also be considered as a virtuoso play, one written to exploit the talents of a particular actor. (See the section of this study guide entitled, *"Cyrano* as a Virtuoso Play," for a more complete examination of this question.) Previously, Rostand had written *La Samaritaine* for Sarah Bernhardt, but that play did not meet with the popular or critical approval which *Cyrano* was to achieve. The fact that *Cyrano* has outlived the actor for whom it was supposedly written, and that many actors have played the lead role successfully surely outweighs the fact that the play might not have been written had not Rostand known an actor who was perfect for the role. More than many artistic efforts, *Cyrano* is a perfect blending of the author's personality, philosophy, and subject, resulting in a work of art that is enjoyable in and for itself, and which has been continually popular since its first performance.

LIFE AND WORKS OF ROSTAND

Edmond Rostand was born in Marseilles, France, on April 1, 1868. When he was twenty-two years old, he married the poet, Rosemond Gerard, and presented his first book, a volume of poems, to her as a wedding gift.

His first play, *Les Romanesques,* which concerned two young lovers, appeared four years later. And the next year, 1895, *La Princesse Lointaine,* was produced. It was the story of the Provençal poet, Rudel. Rostand's next play was *La Samaritaine,* written for the popular French actress, Sarah Bernhardt. Most critics did not like it because one of the characters — and a minor one, at that — was Christ.

Cyrano de Bergerac made its first appearance in 1897 with the actor, Coquelin, in the title role and was presented for 500 consecutive performances. It was the most popular play of the era, and since its first performance there has hardly been a time when it was not in production somewhere in the world. For, although the play is typically French, it is highly popular in other countries, even when it is translated poorly or cut unmercifully.

Rostand's next play, *L'Aiglon,* was about Napoleon's heir. It was too French for foreign audiences, who did not always revere Napoleon as much as did the French, and even in France it was never as popular as *Cyrano.* After its production, Rostand retired to the country for ten years to write *Chantecler.* It received some acclaim, but Paris audiences did not like it nearly so well as they had *Cyrano.*

Rostand was elected to the French Academy at the age of thirty-three, the youngest member at that time. After the production of *Chantecler,* he was raised to Commander of the Legion of Honor and received a "Grand Diploma."

When World War I began, Rostand volunteered for service, but was refused. He consoled himself by writing patriotic poetry. One poem, praising America, was dedicated to Sarah Bernhardt, and another was occasioned by the sinking of the *Lusitania.*

Rostand was never robust, his health being one reason that he retired to the country, and he died in Paris on December 2, 1918. He left one drama, *La Derniere Nuit de Don Juan,* with an unfinished prologue which further illustrated his idea of the unattainable ideal being more desirable than the real or practical.

In the dedication to *Cyrano de Bergerac,* Rostand says that he would like to dedicate the play to the spirit of Cyrano, but since that has passed on to Coquelin, the actor, he dedicates it to Coquelin. Because the actor who plays Cyrano is so very crucial to the success of the play — all the other characters are merely supporting roles — it is fortunate that an actor whom the author considered perfect for the role was able to introduce it.

LIST OF CHARACTERS

Characters whose names are followed by an asterisk are known to have been historical personages.

Cyrano de Bergerac*

The main character of the play. He is a soldier, poet, philosopher, and scientist — a man of immense courage, versatility, and talent. He has an enormous nose and is very sensitive about it. He is an expert swordsman and challenges anyone who mentions his nose. He jealously guards his intellectual freedom, even though he suffers poverty. His integrity and innate nobility of spirit are the theme of the play.

Christian de Neuvillette

Cyrano's comrade-in-arms. A handsome man of noble spirit and generosity. He is in love with Roxane, but unable to express his love in such a way as to be acceptable to her. He is not stupid, but is actually inarticulate.

Roxane (Madeleine Robin)*

The beautiful girl with whom both Cyrano and Christian are in love. She falls in love with Christian's beauty and (though she is unaware of it) Cyrano's mind. She is described as a *précieuse*, which, in seventeenth-century France, meant a person highly affected in language, manners, and dress. To the *précieuse*, what a person *was* was not so important as what he *appeared* to be. Some of them, wishing to appear witty, are said to have rehearsed repartee amongst themselves before going to a party. Molière wrote a play, *Les Précieuse Ridicules*, making fun of them. Christian is afraid that Roxane, being a *précieuse*, would not love a plain-spoken man.

Comte de Guiche*

The villain of the play, Richelieu's nephew, who wants Roxane as his mistress, and wishes her to marry Valvert. Solely for revenge against Christian and Cyrano, he sends the Gascony Guards to almost certain death.

Le Bret*

Cyrano's friend and confidant.

Ragueneau

A poet who runs a bakery shop where other poets congregate.

Lise

Wife of Ragueneau.

Carbon de Castel-Jaloux*

The commander of the Gascony Guards.

Lignière*

A poet, Cyrano's friend. Cyrano single-handedly routs the one hundred men sent to kill Lignière.

Valvert

A *précieuse* who insults Cyrano by referring to his nose. He is the man De Guiche wants Roxane to marry. It is to him that the famous speech of insults is addressed, and it is he with whom Cyrano duels while composing a poem.

Montfleury*

An actor, one of Roxane's suitors. He has incurred Cyrano's displeasure and has been forbidden by Cyrano to act on the stage for three weeks.

Bellerose*

Manager of the theater which Cyrano closes by not allowing Montfleury to act.

Jodelet*

A comedian in the same theater.

Cuigy*
Brissaille* } Friends of Cyrano.

Soeur Marthe
Soeur Claire } Nuns in the convent where Roxane goes to live.

Mère Marguérite de Jésus

Mother Superior at the same convent.

A NOTE ABOUT SCENE DIVISION

Since many of Rostand's devices are confined to and isolated within the space of a scene or two, the authors feel that discussing the play in elements of one entire act at a time would be too broad a basis from which to work, and would lead to confusion on the part of the student. Act II, for example, contains so many dramatic devices, moods, and characters that it would be very difficult to discuss without some reference point, such as scene divisions.

Since many English-language editions of *Cyrano de Bergerac* are not divided into scenes, an explanation of the scene division used here would seem to be in order.

The scene divisions used are the traditional ones: in general, the scenes end or begin when a character of some importance to the plot either exits or makes an entrance. The student using an

English-language translation should have no trouble recognizing the divisions between the scenes if he refers to the exit or entrance of an important character or, simply, to the action described for a particular scene. The student using one of the French-language editions will in all likelihood find that the scene division used here is identical to that used in his copy of the play.

BRIEF SYNOPSIS

The curtain rises to disclose the interior of a theater. Several spectators are present, waiting for the play to begin, and their conversation informs us (erroneously) that this is the famous theater in which Corneille's *Le Cid* was introduced. The play tonight is Baro's *Clorise*, and the leading actor is Montfleury.

Ragueneau and Le Bret enter, and Lignière calls attention to the fashionable people who are present. They wonder where Cyrano is, since he has forbidden Montfleury to act on the stage. When Roxane enters, Christian points her out to Le Bret as the woman with whom he is in love, even though he does not know her name and has never talked to her. Lignière says that De Guiche is also interested in Roxane, and though she is resisting him he is a very powerful and vindictive man. He is also married.

Before the play-within-a-play begins, Christian goes to warn Lignière (who has left the theater) that his latest poem has offended a highly-placed person who has stationed a hundred men near Lignière's street to ambush and murder him.

The curtain rises and Montfleury enters on stage. As he begins to speak, Cyrano's voice interrupts and tells him to leave the stage. Cyrano offers to fight anyone who wishes to defend Montfleury, but there are no volunteers. When the manager of the theater asks Cyrano if he is also going to force him to refund the money of the patrons, Cyrano tosses a bag of gold to the stage, and the manager is happy.

An affected gentleman who wishes to insult Cyrano says, "Your nose is very—large." Cyrano describes to him what a number of different types of people might have said about his nose. Then he says that while they duel, he will compose a *ballade* and thrust on the last line. He proceeds to do just that.

When almost all the spectators have left the theater, Cyrano confesses to Le Bret that he is in love with his cousin, Roxane. Then Roxane's duenna comes in and makes an appointment with Cyrano for the next day. He is ecstatic, and when he learns of Lignière's plight he happily goes off to fight the one hundred men lying in wait for the poet.

The next morning, Cyrano waits for Roxane in Ragueneau's pastry shop. He writes a letter, thinking that he may simply hand it to her when she arrives and leave without waiting for her answer. When she comes, she confesses that she is in love—with Christian. Cyrano, broken-hearted though he is, promises that he will look after Christian for her. All of Paris is talking of his exploit of the previous night in routing the one hundred men sent to murder Lignière. De Guiche comes and offers to be Cyrano's patron, but Cyrano refuses.

Christian joins the Cadets of Gascogne, the famed Gascony Guards, and he and Cyrano become friends. He confesses to Cyrano that he loves Roxane, but that he is afraid that he cannot express himself well enough to win her love. Cyrano gives him the letter which he himself had written to Roxane and tells him to send it to her in his own name. This is the beginning of the deception. Cyrano writes beautiful letters and makes up impassioned speeches which Christian memorizes. Roxane falls in love with Christian's borrowed eloquence.

At last, however, Christian tires of his role as Cyrano's mouthpiece. The company is leaving for the siege of Arras, and before he goes he wants to woo Roxane with his own words. But he has underestimated the strength of her attachment to beautiful language and gets nowhere with her. Cyrano saves the day for him by hiding under the balcony where Roxane stands and whispering words which Christian repeats. Soon, however, Cyrano's enthusiasm makes this unbearable and he speaks aloud — but Roxane does not know that it is he and not Christian who is speaking.

A monk brings a letter from De Guiche to Roxane, saying that he is sending the regiment on ahead, but that he is remaining behind for one night in the expectation of meeting Roxane secretly. Roxane pretends that the letter directs the monk to marry her to Christian immediately, which he does while Cyrano detains De Guiche. The marriage is not consummated, however, because the Guards leave for the front, on the orders of De Guiche, to fight at the siege of Arras.

During the siege, Cyrano finds a way through the lines and risks his life to get letters to Roxane, purportedly from Christian. Much to the surprise of everyone, Roxane appears, bringing food and news, which makes Cyrano's hopes soar. She has come, she says, to confess that at first she loved Christian for his beauty, but that now, because of his letters, she has fallen in love with his spirit and his wonderful mind. This is a much deeper and truer love, and she is ashamed that she has been so shallow.

Christian is an honorable man and he wants Cyrano to tell Roxane the truth. Just as Cyrano is about to do so, Christian's body is carried in; he has been killed by the first shot fired in the battle.

Nearly fifteen years elapse, and we find the mourning Roxane in a convent. She has always carried Christian's last letter next to her heart. Cyrano comes to her each week and gives her a witty resumé of the week's gossip. Today, however, he is late. One of Cyrano's enemies has managed to injure him by having a lackey drop a heavy log on Cyrano's head as he passed beneath a window. Cyrano is mortally wounded, but still comes just at sunset, as always, to give Roxane her news of the outside world. He sits in his usual chair and begins, but then asks to read Christian's last letter. Roxane gives it to him. As he reads, she realizes that it is too dark for him to see the words and that this was the voice she had heard under her balcony on her wedding night. As Cyrano dies, Roxane says that she has loved only once, but has lost her love twice.

SUMMARIES AND COMMENTARIES

ACT I – SCENE 1

Summary

The curtain rises to show the interior of a dimly-lighted theater. Some cavaliers enter without paying and practice fencing; they are followed by two lackeys who sit on the floor and begin gambling; a middle-class man and his son enter; then a pickpocket and his accomplices come in. Through conversations we learn that this is the theater where Corneille's *Le Cid* was first performed, and that the play tonight is Baro's *Clorise*, and that its star is Montfleury.

Commentary

This opening scene is a very good example of two things: the playwright's problem of providing his audience with necessary information, and Rostand's craftsmanship in dealing with the problem. While the novelist can give descriptions, explanations, and background material in many ways, the playwright has only the dialogue and setting – and sometimes the latter must be explained in the dialogue if it is especially significant.

Notice the many types of people – those who come to play cards, to picnic, to flirt, to steal, and even a few honest souls who really want to see the play – whom Rostand introduces in this brief scene. But he is not only describing a cross-section of seventeenth-century French society; he also manages a comment on that society by having the two cavaliers enter the theater without buying tickets. Overall, he gives the very distinct impression to the audience that this is an exciting period in the history of the French theater. And, since the student of French civilization automatically thinks of Corneille, Molière, and Racine when he thinks of seventeenth-century France, what better place to begin a play set in that period than in its most famous theater? (*Le Cid* was not actually introduced in this theater, however.)

Apart from all the information conveyed, there is also the mood of the play, which must be established at the beginning. Rostand does this with his setting, for there is a distinct excitement in a theater before a play just as there is before a symphony or opera when the musicians are tuning their instruments.

If the playwright's problem at the opening of a play were simply that of conveying information and establishing mood, it would be relatively easy to solve. But one must remember that the playwright must not only capture the attention of the audience, but must also hold its interest for the full course of the play. The air of anticipation created by the setting in this scene is added—and the element of suspense is introduced—to the scenes immediately following.

ACT I — SCENES 2-3

Summary

Christian is introduced in Scene 2 by the poet, Lignière. The poet/baker, Ragueneau, enters dressed in his Sunday best, and talks with Lignière. He asks about Cyrano, who has forbidden Montfleury to act, but who has not yet appeared. Ragueneau describes Cyrano's nose as well as his reputation as a swordsman. When Roxane enters the theater, Lignière tells Christian, who has fallen in love with her without knowing her identity, who the lady is. He also tells Christian that De Guiche, who is married to Richelieu's niece and is very powerful, wants Roxane to marry a complaisant courtier, Valvert, so that De Guiche can make her his own mistress. In Lignière's opinion, Christian hasn't a chance with the lady.

After Lignière leaves the theater, Christian learns from a pickpocket that Lignière has written a poem which has offended some powerful person. This highly-placed man plans to have the poet killed and has hired a hundred armed men to waylay Lignière on his way home. Christian goes off to find Lignière and warn him.

Montfleury goes onto the stage and begins his first speech, the prologue of the play, but he is interrupted by the voice of Cyrano telling him to stop. He makes several attempts to continue his speech, but is interrupted by Cyrano each time.

Commentary

It may seem that nothing much happens during the first three scenes. People wander in and out, we are given snatches of conversations, and in Scenes 2 and 3 Christian and Lignière come and go, as does Ragueneau. Actually, these characters are giving us information which we will need later in order to understand the play.

As in Scene 1, there is a variety of characters introduced. The marquis who comments that Christian is handsome enough, but not really in the latest fashion, is an excellent example of the *précieuse* attitude (an attitude, prevalent in seventeenth-century France, that what a person *appeared* to be was more important than what he really *was*). Our knowledge of the marquis — he is vain, and affected in language, manners, and dress — will help us to understand that of Roxane, since she is also one of the *précieuse*.

We are told of the political climate in France and of the worsening relationship with Spain, which prepares us for the later mention of the forthcoming battle of Arras. Duels were fought then, and we discover that an insult in a poem was sufficient cause for murder. We may rightly assume that the theater is important since members of the Academy are present. (The French Academy is composed of very distinguished intellectuals who are, among other duties, the arbiters of the French language.

Their rank is higher than any other in France today — for purposes of seating arrangements at official dinners, for example — though the Academy has lost much of its former prestige.)

By the end of Scene 3 we have been introduced to the three men who are in love with Roxane, and their characters have been explained. Christian is an "honest, brave soldier" who fears that he will not have the words to win her. De Guiche is powerful and arrogant. Cyrano is a noble, brave man, "an exquisite being."

Roxane is introduced as well, and so we have the conflict of the play: De Guiche's interest in Roxane, Christian's love for her, and Cyrano's love for Roxane.

It might, perhaps, be worthy of mention here that Rostand represented most of his characters who have historical counterparts according to the generally reputed personality of the character. Montfleury's obesity was satirized by both Molière and the historical Cyrano, and Lignière refers to him as a "hippopotamus."

The groundwork for the events which occur toward the end of Act I is laid in the knowledge that Lignière is in danger. We are also prepared for Cyrano's appearance: he has a huge nose which no one dares mention to him, even by implication. The interest shown in him arouses our own interest and curiosity. If such a character had appeared without preparation, he might well have seemed merely ridiculous. In other words, we are now prepared for the delightful events in Scene 4.

ACT I – SCENE 4

Summary

Montfleury tries to continue his speech, but is repeatedly interrupted by Cyrano. The audience jeers Cyrano, who offers to fight anyone who will come forward in Montfleury's defense, but no one comes. Montfleury leaves the stage. The theater manager points out to Cyrano that if he does not allow the play to proceed, the manager will have to refund the money to the patrons. Cyrano tosses a sack of gold to him, which is obviously more than adequate to cover the loss. Cyrano is not worried by the fact that Montfleury has a powerful patron who may be angry at Cyrano's preventing the performance.

The vicomte, Valvert, says to Cyrano, "Your nose is, hmm . . . is . . . very . . . hmm . . . big." This leads to one of the memorable moments of the play in which Cyrano, with great wit and charm, suggests what many types of people might say about his nose. After this tirade by Cyrano, De Guiche tries to lead the vicomte away, but the foolish man delays long enough to sneer at Cyrano for not wearing gloves. Cyrano replies that his elegances are moral ones. Then he announces that he will fight a duel with the vicomte and that, while they are fighting, he will compose a *ballade* (a poem consisting of three stanzas of eight lines each, concluding with a four-line refrain). At the end of the refrain, he says, he will end the duel with a thrust. He does exactly as he has promised.

When the hall is almost empty, Le Bret asks why Cyrano has not eaten dinner. He confesses that he has no money. Le Bret asks about the sack of gold that Cyrano threw to the theater manager, and Cyrano confesses that that was his month's income — he has nothing left. "What foolishness," says Le Bret. "But what a beautiful gesture!" Cyrano replies.

Commentary

The first three scenes of the first act have accomplished, among other things, the setting of the play and the introduction of nearly all of the major characters, including Cyrano. But Cyrano does not appear on the stage during these three scenes. All we know about him — who and what he is, as well as the size of his nose — comes from the dialogue of no less than half a dozen other characters. This preparation is extremely important, for if we were not so well prepared beforehand — if, for instance, Cyrano were to be visible on stage at the rise of the opening curtain — our reaction to this apparently ludicrous character would be completely different from what it is. As it is, we have heard a great deal about Cyrano in these early scenes, and Scene 3 ends with Cyrano on stage (but hidden by the crowd) speaking to Montfleury.

Scene 4 begins with Cyrano making himself visible to the audience. Notice that there is not necessarily a curtain nor any break in the action between scenes. And here is an excellent example of Rostand's dramatic technique. When a major character makes an important entrance, the eyes, as well as the interest of the audience must be directed to that character. A standard device for accomplishing this is by having a minor character precede the major character on stage and announce his arrival. Rostand's device is enormously more effective. Cyrano's presence on stage is indicated only when he speaks his first line to Montfleury, and suspense is heightened as the audience tries to locate the speaker. In case some of the audience still do not know where to look for Cyrano, Rostand has Cyrano raise his arm and wave his cane. *Now* we know exactly where he is, and the attention of the audience is riveted to the spot. And *now* we are finally allowed to see the man for whose entrance we have been so well prepared.

This long scene is not only exciting from both the intellectual and physical standpoints, but it serves to refine our knowledge of Cyrano's character. And it is his character and personality which make most of the events in the play seem real and logical regardless of how unlikely they might appear otherwise. In other words, given Cyrano's character, there is a "willing suspension of disbelief" on the part of the audience.

Cyrano's extreme sensitivity about his nose (the historical Cyrano is supposed to have been just as touchy) is made clear when he challenges the vicomte to a duel and doubly insults him by besting him in the duel and composing a poem at the same time.

Cyrano is highly intelligent, talented, brave, impetuous, and sensitive. He is more than that: after the duel we learn that he has no money left. His comment that tossing the bag of gold onto the stage to reimburse the theater manager was a beautiful gesture tells us that the "beau geste" means more to him than bread. He is extremely idealistic and has a very dramatic temperament.

From the discussion about the patron of Montfleury, we learn that all artists are expected to have a patron—one who supports his protégé with money and position. Cyrano has no patron. He stands alone, beholden to no man, independent, unafraid and unprotected.

ACT I—SCENES 5-7

Summary

As Cyrano eats the frugal "meal" provided by the adoring little orange-girl, Le Bret warns him that his rash actions are making powerful enemies, but Cyrano refuses to be seriously concerned. He says, "I have decided to be admirable in everything." He then confesses that he is in love with his cousin Roxane, but that he is so ugly that he is afraid to try to win her hand. The only thing he fears is having his nose laughed at; for her to laugh at him would be a blow he dare not risk.

In Scene 6 Roxane's duenna enters the theater and asks Cyrano to meet Roxane. Elated, he makes an appointment to meet her at Ragueneau's pastry shop the next morning at seven o'clock. Cyrano is ecstatic; he feels invincible; he feels that he needs to fight whole armies.

Brissaille enters with the drunken Lignière, saying that Lignière is in trouble. Lignière explains that his poem has gotten him into difficulties; Cyrano orders his entourage to follow and watch, but not to interfere. He will defend Lignière himself because he once saw his friend perform a lovely romantic gesture. Cyrano leaves the stage twenty paces ahead of the rest—officers, comedians, actresses, and musicians—pausing only to explain that it was necessary to send a hundred men to kill Lignière because it is well known that he is a friend of Cyrano's.

Commentary

In these three scenes Rostand finishes giving the audience the problem on which the plot turns. We already know that Christian is in love with Roxane and that he is afraid that he is not sufficiently eloquent to win her hand. Now we have the knowledge that the fabulous Cyrano also loves her—and he certainly has the language at his command to win a woman of her type—but he fears that she would not love him because of his physical oddity: his enormous nose.

The act ends on a very hopeful note, as far as Cyrano's love for Roxane is concerned. We see how a little encouragement in this direction increases his already monumental dash and daring. He gladly goes to fight a hundred men. The fact that Lignière is in trouble was carefully prepared for earlier, so this is no surprise. And we know that Cyrano is just the sort who would gaily and pompously lead his admirers to watch him fight a hundred men.

Although Cyrano does not appear until Act I, Scene 3—and actually only his voice is heard in Scene 3—he has been described, and we are thoroughly prepared for him. Also, by the time Cyrano makes a physical appearance in Scene 4, Rostand has so completely established the character that we are more delighted than surprised by his extravagances. Rostand has, in addition, established so much sympathy for his main character that we hope that Roxane is going to confess her love for him and not merely warn him of some plot or give him some other cousinly message. This is one of Rostand's most artful strokes, and one of his secrets of making fantastic, romantic nonsense believable.

ACT II—SCENES 1-2

Summary

Act II takes place in the pastry shop owned by Ragueneau, who was introduced in Act I. Ragueneau's wife, Lise, has more business sense and less love of poetry than her husband—she has made sacks out of the poems his friends have left in payment for food. Two children make a small purchase, and Lise wraps their pastries in the pages of poetry. When his wife is not looking, Ragueneau calls the children back and trades them three more pastries for the poems.

Commentary

These short scenes serve to establish the personalities of Ragueneau and his wife, Lise, as well as the fact that there is a conflict between them. Ragueneau seems to be almost a caricature of Cyrano—a man who loves the gallant gesture, the bravado of the soldier, and the sensitivity of the poet. Ragueneau reappears throughout the play as a friend and admirer of Cyrano, and since Act III will open with the tale of Ragueneau's own drama, Rostand very economically prepares us for that in these scenes.

Ragueneau is a "utility" character in the play. In Act I, he gives the audience various bits of important information; in Act II, he provides an appropriate setting for the occurrences which take place in that act; in Act IV, he serves in the capacity of coachman; and in Act V, he is the necessary old friend of Cyrano. How much more interesting it is for these to be combined into one character with a personality and history instead of being portrayed by a series of faceless actors. Moreover, the preparation for Ragueneau's tale gives the audience an opportunity to become accustomed to, and to enjoy, the setting of the little pastry shop—which, incidentally, Rostand envisioned as a very complicated and interesting set. If he had had any really important action take place at the very beginning of the act, it might well have failed to make the proper impression upon an audience absorbed in the scenery.

ACT II—SCENES 3-4

Summary

Cyrano enters and Ragueneau congratulates him on the duel in the theater the night before. But Cyrano is not interested in anything except his meeting with Roxane. He asks Ragueneau to clear the place out when he gives the signal, and Ragueneau agrees. A musketeer enters who will be mentioned again later.

The poets come in, for their "first meal," as Lise says. They are all excited about the feat of the evening before — one man against a hundred, and no one knows who the brave one was. Cyrano is writing a love letter to Roxane and is not at all interested in the conversation around him. He does not sign the letter, because he plans to give it to Roxane himself.

The poets flatter Ragueneau by asking for his latest poetic effort — a recipe in rhyme.

Cyrano constantly asks the time, and the hour finally arrives for his meeting with Roxane. The poets are rushed to another room so that Cyrano can see her alone.

Commentary

These scenes contain several elements of interest: Lise's sarcasm about the poets, the comedy of Ragueneau's recipe in verse, and the fact that the poets are buzzing with talk of Cyrano's various exploits of the previous evening. Cyrano himself, however, is the most interesting element. He is concerned only with the letter he is writing to Roxane — the one he has carried in his heart for years — and in the fact that he will soon see her and at last declare his love for her. He cares about nothing else. The brave hero is as excited as a schoolboy.

In the first act, our attention has been directed to Cyrano's bravado and his true courage, but now we are seeing a completely different facet of his personality. He is so nervous about his forthcoming confrontation with Roxane that he simply ignores the opportunity to submit himself to the adulation of the poets.

ACT II – SCENES 5-6

Summary

Cyrano fills the "poetry-sacks" with pastry for Roxane's duenna, who goes into the street to eat, then he and Roxane, who are cousins, reminisce about their childhood games. She tenderly bandages his injured hand with her handkerchief while she tells him shyly that she is in love with someone in his regiment. Cyrano's hopes rise. Then she adds that this man is young, fearless — and handsome.

Cyrano asks if she has spoken with him. "Only with our eyes," she replies. But Cyrano asks, "What if he is a savage — uncultured, unlettered?" Roxane declares that no one with such beautiful hair could fail to be eloquent.

She has come to Cyrano because Christian, her love, has joined Cyrano's regiment. She knows that it is the custom to provoke an outsider to a duel, since the regiment is composed entirely of men from Gascony. She wants Cyrano to protect Christian, and he promises to do so.

Commentary

In the beginning of this scene, Rostand very skillfully builds up the hopes of Cyrano and the audience. Roxane commences quite naturally with childhood memories and, until she pronounces the word, "handsome," there is really no reason to believe that she is not going to confess her love for Cyrano. This, of course, makes Cyrano's disappointment more acute. Promising to protect Christian is a bitter pill for him to swallow. This promise, however, is preparation for what is to follow.

Cyrano never seems to feel that Roxane should be any different than she is — only that *his* nose is at fault. Since he and Roxane have known each other so long, Cyrano may see qualities in his lady love which are not readily apparent to others. It does not seem possible that one of his intelligence and sensitivity should be in love with a woman totally committed to the shallowness and pretentiousness of the *précieuse* philosophy.

ACT II — SCENES 7-8

Summary

The Gascony Guards enter, proud of Cyrano. There is also a poet who wants to immortalize the exploit, and a newspaper editor who wants to interview Cyrano. The little pastry shop is suddenly full and noisy. Cyrano, of course, cares nothing for poets and reporters. When Le Bret asks about his interview with Roxane, Cyrano simply tells him to be quiet. De Guiche, Richelieu's powerful nephew who wants Roxane for his mistress, offers the services of himself and his uncle. Cyrano refuses, though he has written a play which he would like to see produced. As De Guiche leaves, he asks Cyrano if he knows of Don Quixote. Cyrano acknowledges that he recognizes himself. De Guiche tells him that the arm of the windmill could cause his downfall, but Cyrano refuses to be intimidated.

Le Bret chides Cyrano for throwing away such a brilliant opportunity. Cyrano describes the life of a protégé in disparaging terms. He wants to be free, to sing, to dream. He still refuses to discuss Roxane.

Commentary

Scene 7 gets the cadets on stage and shows their admiration of Cyrano. Cyrano, in refusing De Guiche's offer so cavalierly, is in a sense throwing away another bag of gold. This, however, is more than an extravagant gesture; it is also a dangerous one since De Guiche is a powerful man who does not like to be crossed.

Cyrano's impassioned defense to Le Bret of intellectual freedom is a beautiful speech, altogether in character, and as impractical as Ragueneau's attitude toward the poets. One might say, however, that it is just such impractical attitudes as this one

in the play which have caused *Cyrano* to be continuously popular through the years. It is these ideas which have caused men
to rebel, even up to our present day.

ACT II – SCENES 9-10

Summary

Christian enters and talks with the Guards, and the other
cadets tell him that he must under no circumstances mention or
imply the word "nose" in Cyrano's presence. The cadets ask
Cyrano to tell them about the fights of the evening before. Averse
as he was to telling reporters or poets about his exploits, he
enjoys telling his friends. While Cyrano is talking, Christian
continually interrupts him by interjecting the word "nose" into
the story. Cyrano becomes more and more furious but, knowing
that Christian is the man whom he has promised to protect, he
cannot give vent to his anger. At last, he can stand it no longer.
He sends everyone out and explains that he is Roxane's cousin.
Christian confesses that he is afraid that he will lose Roxane because he cannot speak and write well – he is only a simple
soldier. Roxane is so refined that she will surely not love him.
Cyrano says that together, with Christian's looks and Cyrano's
genius, they make one perfect hero. Roxane will suffer no disappointment. He gives Christian the unsigned letter he had
written, telling him to send it as his own – he has but to sign it.

Commentary

Rostand establishes once and for all that Christian is no
coward by having him try very hard to impress the cadets. He
has been warned about the subject of Cyrano's nose, so he does
his best to provoke the famous swordsman to a duel. There is
humor in Cyrano's dilemma.

Cyrano's guess proves to be true. Christian confesses, in
effect, that his brain-power is not the equal of his physical beauty.
Cyrano generously gives the letter to him, beginning the deceit
which will last for nearly fifteen years. Rostand brings this

ridiculous situation about so carefully that it seems almost logical. He has prepared us for everything. The unsigned letter is at hand.

Is Cyrano being generous? Does he merely want Roxane to have what she wants? Does he really think that she could be happy as the wife of the brave but simple soldier?'On the other hand, perhaps he really meant his defense of freedom speech in Scene 8. Perhaps he realizes subconsciously that what he needs is not a wife, but an unrequited love. His motive is one we will never know. Rostand nowhere implies that Cyrano ever adopts any of the false values of the *précieuse* and we must assume that his conscious motive is pure and noble. Perhaps he feels that Christian is worthy of Roxane. Or maybe his disappointment is so acute that for the moment he feels defeated. While there are many possible explanations, the play is a better one for leaving a few questions unanswered.

ACT II – SCENE 11

Summary

The cadets re-enter, and much to their surprise find Christian still alive. The musketeer, deciding that one can now make fun of Cyrano's nose with impunity, tries his hand at the game. Cyrano knocks him down.

Commentary

Throughout this act, Cyrano's emotions have run the gamut from elation to depression, and the emotions of the audience have followed in close pursuit. In addition to setting up the situation of the play, Rostand has gotten his audience involved with Cyrano, the man. The playwright has made us hope that his main character's dream of love will come true, only to have those hopes dashed to earth. And he has added the irony that Cyrano must not only protect the man who is taking his love from him, but must also help him to win the girl through deception. And

28

so, by the end of the act we are in need of the comic relief furnished by this scene and the two which precede it.

In the previous two scenes, Cyrano is caught in the dilemma of having to accept the insults of the man he has sworn to protect. This internal struggle which goes on as he tries to recount his exploits over Christian's interruptions is a source of high humor for the audience. And the act ends on an even more humorous note when the musketeer misinterprets the situation. Since Cyrano does not kill the musketeer, but simply knocks him down for his insult, it is obvious that Rostand's intention was to end the act on the much-needed light note.

ACT III – SCENE 1

Summary

Act III, entitled "Roxane's Kiss," takes place in the street under Roxane's balcony. It opens with Ragueneau telling Roxane's duenna that his wife, Lise, ran off with the musketeer. He tried to hang himself, but Cyrano saved him and brought him to Roxane to be a steward in her household.

Cyrano enters, followed by musicians whom he keeps correcting. He explains that he won them for a day with a bet over a fine point of grammar. Roxane tells Cyrano that Christian is a genius: he will be quiet and distracted for a moment, then say the most beautiful things. Cyrano teases her about some of Christian's speeches.

Commentary

The fact that Cyrano saved Ragueneau's life is characteristic of Cyrano. Lise's defection is a logical result of the relationship shown in Act II between her and Ragueneau (even the musketeer was introduced – see Act II, Scenes 3 and 4, as well as Scene 11). This enables Rostand to keep Ragueneau in the play and gives the baker good reason to be a loyal friend to Cyrano.

Note that Cyrano, the Renaissance man, has won the musicians in a dispute over a point of grammar—("I was right, of course.")—and is now correcting the musicians. He knows grammar and music, writes poetry, and is a superb swordsman. New facets of his personality, and new abilities, are continually being shown to us.

Cyrano enjoys teasing Roxane about Christian's (really his own) beautiful speeches, and hearing her hotly defend each word. Though writing for someone else, he still has an author's pride in his creation. It seems that this is a game to him, a way to exercise his fertile brain and facile wit, and that he gives little or no thought to the consequences. He may, of course, be convinced that since they do love each other, as each has confessed to him, playing Cupid is the noblest, most generous and extravagant gesture he can make. He is, after all, a modest man in some ways.

ACT III — SCENES 2-3

Summary

De Guiche enters and tells Roxane that he has come to say goodbye. He has been placed in command of Cyrano's regiment. She tells him that if he really wants to hurt Cyrano, he should leave him and the other cadets behind, while the rest of the regiment goes on to glorious victory. De Guiche sees in this a sign that Roxane loves him (De Guiche) and suggests a rendezvous at a monastery. She makes De Guiche believe she is consenting; she has managed to keep Christian out of the war.

Cyrano comes out of the house and asks Roxane on what subject she will ask Christian to speak tonight. She replies that tonight he must improvise on the subject of love.

Commentary

For the sake of Christian, Roxane plays the coquette with De Guiche, and very skillfully. We are shown how powerful

De Guiche is, and how much vengeance he would take for a slight, for Cyrano has only refused De Guiche's offer to be his patron. He does not hesitate to use this threat of revenge against Cyrano (and Christian, too, though he does not know about Christian's relationship with Roxane) to influence Roxane.

When Roxane tells Cyrano that Christian's subject for the evening will be to improvise on love, he sees an opportunity to work in all the beautiful phrases he has been saving up for just such an occasion.

ACT III – SCENE 4

Summary

Christian refuses to memorize speeches tonight. He is tired of pretense: he knows enough, he says, to take a woman in his arms. He knows that Roxane loves him, and refuses to continue this uncomfortable and demeaning role.

Commentary

We have already seen, in Act II, that Christian is no coward, though he lacks the facility with words that Roxane demands of a lover. Here we see that he has moral courage as well. Cyrano is not the only noble character in this play. If Christian had never protested the deception which he and Cyrano are perpetrating upon Roxane, we would think much less of him, and it is necessary that he be a noble idealist, though of course much less so than Cyrano. Without this protest, he would seem a rather despicable character. This scene makes his plight a tragic one, for he feels that he can accomplish his purpose by means of his own capabilities when, in fact, he cannot. Thus, the scene also raises the situation above the comic or the opportunistic aspect it might otherwise have had.

ACT III – SCENES 5-7

Summary

Christian tells Roxane, "I love you." "That," she replies, "is the theme. Embroider."

Of course, poor Christian can think of nothing else to say. Roxane goes inside in disgust. Christian asks Cyrano to help him. Cyrano hides under Roxane's balcony and whispers to Christian, who repeats the words aloud to Roxane. At last, Cyrano is carried away and speaks aloud eloquently himself, but Roxane still believes it is Christian who is doing the speaking.

Commentary

Second only to the famous one in *Romeo and Juliet,* this is probably the most famous balcony scene in literature. In fact, one wonders if Rostand might not have had in mind a parody of Shakespeare's well-known scene as he began writing this. At any rate, it contains many elements of interest. There is some amusement in Cyrano's whispering to Christian. There is poignancy in poor Cyrano's winning Roxane's love, not for himself, but for Christian. There is irony in the fact that he talks to her of honesty, of doing away with artificiality. We wonder if Cyrano could have won her love if he had written eloquent letters in his own name and spoken for himself—and perhaps brought her to a more mature sense of values.

ACT III – SCENES 8-10

Summary

A monk comes by, looking for Roxane's house, and Cyrano misdirects him. Christian wants Roxane's kiss, climbs the balcony, and kisses her. The monk returns. He is delivering a letter from De Guiche to Roxane. De Guiche has sent his regiment on but has stayed behind himself. The letter instructs her that he is coming to see her. She tells the monk that De Guiche's letter orders that she and Christian be married immediately. She pretends that this is against her will and the monk is completely convinced. The monk, Christian, and Roxane go inside for the ceremony, while Cyrano waits outside to divert De Guiche.

Commentary

It might be worthwhile at this point to remind the reader briefly about the traditional practices of scene division. This section, as well as the preceding section, describes portions of the play which are very closely knit. Then, why divide each of the sections into three scenes? As mentioned earlier, it is traditional in drama to begin and end scenes with the entrance and exit of a reasonably important character, and such is the case here. Though there are no real interruptions in these sections, there are certain entrances and exits which would be marked as scene divisions in some texts. If the student is using a text without scene divisions, he can easily locate the portion of an act dealt with in the summaries by simply comparing the actions described with his text.

Roxane is very quick-witted in these scenes. She seems a little hasty in her wish to marry a man she sent away a short time earlier because he could not embroider upon the theme of love. The fact that De Guiche is pressing her may have something to do with her decision. At any rate, Rostand has managed to make the whole thing quite believable. We already know of De Guiche's desire for Roxane and of his power. This seems a simple and logical way out of all the difficulties Roxane and Christian would have if they married in a more conventional manner. It is necessary that they be married to explain Roxane's behavior in Acts IV and V.

ACT III – SCENES 11-12

Summary

Cyrano has climbed to the top of the wall, and when De Guiche enters, Cyrano swings from a branch and drops down in front of him. He tells De Guiche that he came from the moon and asks where he is. In spite of himself, De Guiche is amused. When Cyrano says that he has invented six ways to travel to the moon, De Guiche is curious enough to listen to what they are. Then, after telling him the six ways, Cyrano says, in his own voice, that the quarter of an hour is up, and the marriage completed. He believes there is nothing De Guiche can do about the marriage. De Guiche, however, gains revenge by sending the cadets to the front immediately.

Commentary

The brilliant bit of nonsense in Scene 11 is an opportunity for Cyrano to show off yet another of his interests — science. But, before the reader begins to feel that Rostand is exaggerating Cyrano's varied interests, he should remember that among the many talents of the historical Cyrano was that of writing science-fiction.

Poor Cyrano not only wins the lady for Christian, but must stall De Guich while the couple is being married. He promises that "Christian" will write to her often. Since Rostand has De Guiche on the scene, has prepared us for his anger, and has already introduced the war, he encounters no difficulty in separating the young couple immediately, before they have a moment alone together. Thus, Roxane never has an opportunity to know her husband without Cyrano's words to make him seem more facile of tongue.

ACT IV — SCENE 1

Summary

This act takes place in the camp of the Gascony Guards at the siege of Arras. The soldiers are all suffering from hunger, for while the French are besieging Arras, the Spanish have encircled them and no supplies can be brought to them through the lines. Cyrano, at great risk to his life, has found a way to get across the lines and he does so in order to send "Christian's" letters to

Roxane. The reason that he does not bring food on any of these trips is that it would be too bulky for him to carry and still be able to evade the Spaniards. Cyrano says that he thinks there must be a change soon, that the company will either eat or die: the Spanish are planning something.

Commentary

Act III has been a light, often humorous, act. Now, however, the mood undergoes a very definite change. This scene sets that mood by showing us the state of the war and indicating that the situation at Arras is very serious. The atmosphere of gloom deepens throughout the act, with only one touch of lightness.

How typical that Cyrano's dangerous journeys through the enemy lines are made for spiritual and not physical reasons! Keeping the promise of frequent letters, which he made for Christian in Act III, Scene 12, does not seem sufficient justification, especially since he cannot bring food back with him. (And we can be sure that, with his friends approaching starvation on the other side of the lines, he would not avail himself of the opportunity to eat.) Perhaps he feels that once the war is over he will never have another chance to tell Roxane of his love, and he wants to do that more than anything else, even if he must sign Christian's name to his own letters.

ACT IV – SCENES 2-3

Summary

The cadets complain of hunger. Cyrano tries to entertain them with his wit, but when even he cannot cheer them up, he asks an old piper to play some familiar Provencal songs for them and speaks to them of home. When Carbon protests that Cyrano is making them cry, Cyrano responds that it is nobler to cry from homesickness than it is to cry from hunger, because homesickness is moral and hunger is physical.

Commentary

These scenes provide Rostand the opportunity to work in some of the lovely folk songs from southern France, and they also point up Cyrano's leadership among the cadets. It is he who is resourceful enough to cheer them. The observation that it is nobler to cry from homesickness than hunger is an interesting bit of philosophy. It is also good psychology as well, since a desire to live to return home is more likely to sustain them than self-pity.

ACT IV—SCENE 4

Summary

De Guiche enters. He says that he knows the cadets do not like him. The cadets continue smoking and playing cards as if they were not paying any attention to De Guiche. They do not want him to know how miserable they are. He tells them of his action in the war the day before. Cyrano, however, knows every detail. He knows that when De Guiche's life was in danger, he flung off his officer's scarf so he would not be recognized. Cyrano picked up the scarf, and now exposes De Guiche's cowardice by producing it. De Guiche mounts the parapet and waves the scarf, explaining that, with the aid of a spy, he has arranged for the Spanish to attack at the position from which he signals. At the same time, the French armies will mount their own attack against the weakest position of the Spaniards. De Guiche admits that, by ordering the attack on the Gascony Guards, he serves both the king and his own rancour.

Christian says that he would like to put his love for Roxane into one last letter. Cyrano hands him a letter he has ready. Christian notices that a tear has splashed on the letter, and Cyrano explains that the letter was so beautiful that he himself was carried away with emotion.

The sentinel announces that a carriage approaches and the cadets line up, preparing a salute.

Commentary

De Guiche is certainly not a pleasant character, but he is at least honest. The attack which he has arranged for at this position will probably turn into a massacre of the Gascons. The cadets show their dislike for him quite openly, and Cyrano has shown that his own courage exceeds that of De Guiche by retrieving De Guiche's scarf from the most dangerous part of the battlefield. It is another touch of irony in the play that Cyrano's displaying of the scarf is the action which makes De Guiche come to a definite conclusion about inviting the attack.

Rostand has established that Cyrano manages to get through the lines to send letters, but at very great risk on his life. Surely, if it were at all possible to get food in, he would do so. Thus, when a coachman arrives, declaring that he is in the service of the king of France, it is certainly cause for amazement.

This business is ridiculous, but absolutely essential for the development of the plot. Rostand does it about as well as it could be done, inasmuch as he thoroughly prepares the audience for everything explainable and makes a thorough surprise of what is not logical.

ACT IV—SCENES 5-7

Summary

When the carriage comes to a halt, everyone is astonished to see Roxane alight from it. She has charmed her way through the Spanish lines and gaily explains that this siege has gone on too long. De Guiche and Cyrano try to convince her to leave, but she refuses.

The cadets are introduced to Roxane. She gives them her dainty handkerchief to use as a banner. She has managed to bring a carriage-load of gourmet food with her and, with Ragueneau's help, she dispenses it to the cadets. They eat hungrily, but hide the food when De Guiche returns.

De Guiche announces that he has brought a cannon for the cadets. He says that if Roxane will not leave the encampment and return to safety he will stay, too. Cyrano cautions Christian to remember about all the letters written to Roxane in Christian's behalf.

Commentary

Though absolutely necessary to the plot, this is one of the weakest points of the play. The only thing more ridiculous than Roxane's arrival on the scene is her explanation of how she managed the feat. The student of drama—particularly the student of playwriting—could learn a great deal about dramatic structure by attempting to re-write Act IV in summary form. The problem would be to accomplish the same thing as Rostand in terms of plot, but to avoid the more far-fetched elements such as those contained in these scenes.

At this point in the play, it would be well to re-assess Roxane's behavior. It is possible that one might mistakenly believe her to be shallow, frivolous, and self-centered. But this is not true. Although she is all these things on the surface, she is also extremely intelligent and sensitive. It is true that she came to see Christian, but apparently an equally important reason was to bring the food for the company of cadets. She flirted her way through the Spanish lines and concealed the food very cleverly. Also, she was not shallow when she managed to keep Christian's regiment at home for a time and deceive De Guiche. It must be remembered that she truly does appreciate Cyrano's poetry, and because of the letters he has written, true love has bloomed within her for the first time. We are seeing a new dimension of Roxane, quite different from the *précieuse* we were introduced to.

De Guiche and Cyrano have one thing in common—they both love the same woman; only for her do they join forces. In Scene 7, Rostand begins to change the audience's mind about De Guiche and show us that he is not really all bad. He is at least sincere in his concern for Roxane. If she insists upon staying for what he is sure will be her death, he, too, will commit suicide by remaining with her. Thus does Rostand begin to imply that, at least at this point in his life, De Guiche's heart is filled more with love for Roxane than with lust. Rostand then brings the audience's attention back from the war to the letters.

ACT IV — SCENE 8

Summary

Roxane tells Christian that she has made the dangerous journey to come to him because of the letters which he has written to her. She says that she began to know his mind and soul the night when he spoke to her under her balcony. And the letters were so powerful and so sincere, that she now wants to ask his pardon for loving him only for his physical beauty. She feels now that that was an insult, for his mind and his spirit are so much more beautiful. In reading his letters she has learned to love him for better reasons, more deeply than before. His physical appearance now means nothing to her.

Commentary

This is the reason that Roxane has to make an appearance on the battlefield. Without this scene the play would be meaningless. Christian *must* learn that it is Cyrano whom Roxane actually loves. We also now discover that Roxane's character has begun to undergo a very definite change. She is capable of more maturity than Cyrano gave her credit for. His persuasive powers are greater than he knew, for he did not dare trust his ability to woo her for himself. And now she is married to Christian.

ACT IV — SCENE 9

Summary

Christian tells Cyrano that Roxane loves not him, but Cyrano, for she loves the author of the letters and the man who spoke to her under her balcony. Since she is unaware of this, Christian wants Roxane to be told the truth so that she may choose between them. He calls Roxane and exits, leaving Cyrano to explain the fraudulent situation. Cyrano begins to unravel the story, but just when his hopes are aroused, Christian's body is carried on stage; he has been killed by the first bullet fired in the battle. This bullet also destroys Cyrano's hopes; he can never tell Roxane the truth now, especially after she discovers a letter on Christian's body. It is addressed to her, covered with Christian's blood and, although Roxane does not know it, Cyrano's tears.

Commentary

Christian has all the virtues except eloquence. He behaves nobly. One wonders why he never before guessed that Cyrano loves Roxane. Perhaps he was blinded by his own love for her, or perhaps we should credit Cyrano's glib tongue and forceful personality with the successful deception.

Christian has to die, of course. Cyrano's despair over an unrequited love can hold an audience's attention for only a limited amount of time. And what sort of climax can the play have if the war ends with Cyrano, Christian, and Roxane all still alive? What sort of relationship would develop then between these three? Rostand very cleverly makes De Guiche, Roxane, and Christian show the noblest and most mature sides of their characters in this act, and at this moment we are especially sympathetic to Christian.

ACT V – SCENE 1

Summary

The final act takes place in the courtyard of a convent. The sisters are awaiting Cyrano's arrival. We learn that he is poor, often hungry, and that he visits Roxane, who took refuge here after Christian's death, every Saturday.

Commentary

This subdued scene, which takes place more than fourteen years after the incidents which closed Act IV, gives the audience an opportunity to become accustomed to the setting and to learn the situation. As noted elsewhere, this is a characteristic quality of the scenes which open the various acts of the play.

The nuns explain the situation as it has existed for nearly fifteen years. They also give a clear and very endearing picture of Cyrano's visits to Roxane, who is still grieving for Christian. The nuns love Cyrano and enjoy telling him their little pecadillos and being teased by him. They know that, while he may not be a good Catholic (could Cyrano ever conform to anything except his own notions of chivalry?), he is the best and noblest of men. He takes it upon himself to bring a smile to Roxane's face. Cyrano is a ray of sunshine in her life and in the lives of the nuns. He hides his poverty with his pride, his wit, and his charm.

ACT V – SCENES 2-3

Summary

Roxane is talking to De Guiche, who is now the Duc de Grammont. Roxane has lived in the convent in mourning for all these years, always carrying "Christian's last letter" next to her heart. Le Bret enters. They worry about Cyrano, who always seems to be cold, hungry, and alone, and whose writings have made him new enemies.

De Guiche admits that, in spite of all he has and all that Cyrano lacks, Cyrano in his poverty is the better and happier man. In other words, things of the spirit are of more value and are nobler than material things. De Guiche then calls Le Bret aside and tells him that Cyrano is in danger of his life.

As Roxane walks with the duke, Ragueneau enters hurriedly. He tells Le Bret that Cyrano has had an "accident" — someone has dropped a heavy log of wood on his head as he passed beneath a window. Ragueneau has carried Cyrano to his room. The two men hurry to him.

Commentary

We learn that, while De Guiche has mellowed, Cyrano is much the same. Independent, outspoken, fearless, witty, he has antagonized many important men with his satires. This is reminiscent of Lignière, in Act I. Ragueneau is still the "utility" character, a faithful friend of Cyrano.

Notice that De Guiche praises Cyrano before he hears of the accident. The friends (and the former enemy) have been faithful to each other. While this is some fourteen years later, it is worth remembering that Roxane must have been quite young at the beginning of the play and could hardly be more than about thirty-five years old now. In those times, when the aging process was faster and the life expectancy much shorter, she would be, at the very least, approaching middle age. Nonetheless, De Guiche and Cyrano still look upon Roxane as a beautiful and desirable woman. There is irony in the fact that the letter which Roxane carries next to her heart is the one which Cyrano gave to Christian in Act IV, and which was found on Christian's body.

ACT V – SCENE 4

Summary

Roxane is alone. Two nuns bring Cyrano's favorite chair and place it under the tree in the courtyard. The leaves are falling and Cyrano is late. This is so unusual that Roxane is worried about him. Then a sister announces his arrival.

Commentary

As Cyrano was a faithful writer, he is now a faithful visitor. His weekly visits to Roxane considerably brighten her self-imposed retirement. The nuns also obviously look forward to seeing Cyrano. He is the sort of man who could be very popular and tactful, and the nuns' attitudes toward him are altogether in character. One may also contrast Cyrano's constancy with the apparent neglect which De Guiche has shown Roxane.

Rostand uses some rather obvious symbolism here. The leaves are falling from the tree, indicating the approach of winter when everything dies, at least for a while. Cyrano, too, is fast approaching his end.

ACT V – SCENE 5

Summary

Roxane works on her tapestry, and does not notice that Cyrano is pale. Sister Marthe, whom he teases as usual, thinks that his pallor is caused by hunger. Cyrano begins his witty, amusing account of the week's gossip, then nearly faints for a moment. He asks to see Roxane's last letter from Christian. Roxane gives it to him, and he reads it aloud. Roxane recognizes the voice which she heard under her balcony so long ago. She realizes that it is dark, that Cyrano could not be reading the letter but must be quoting from memory. She understands the deception at last, and knows that it is Cyrano whom she loved.

Commentary

Rostand has carefully prepared the audience for the significance of the letter. The scene is poignant, thoroughly romantic, and thoroughly in character for Cyrano. He could not have told her earlier that the husband she mourned was not the author of the letters or of the romantic speeches. He has lived his life as he wished, content with seeing her once each Saturday, and free to write what he wanted. Roxane cannot be told the truth, she must divine it. Through all the years she has been faithful to Christian (really to Cyrano), and this must have pleased Cyrano.

ACT V – SCENE 6

Summary

Le Bret and Ragueneau enter. Cyrano says that he has barely missed everything in life – including a noble death. Ragueneau says that Molière has stolen a scene from one of Cyrano's plays and that it has been very well received. Cyrano says that that is the way his life has been — Molière has the genius, Christian had the beauty. Cyrano compares himself and Roxane to the fable of "Beauty and the Beast," then thanks Roxane for her friendship. He dies praising his unsullied white plume — his integrity.

Commentary

Cyrano did not lack any quality which would have given him a more successful life, but he lacked the right combination of qualities. He was notably self-confident with a sword or pen in his hand, but was so ashamed of his ugliness that he did not try to win Roxane. He did not lack genius, since we see that the stolen act of his play is very popular, but he refused to try to get along with the "right" people.

In fact, Cyrano prized his independence, his unique and unfettered style, above any worldly success. Just as it is nobler to weep for a spiritual reason than a physical one, so it was nobler to live for his moral and spiritual principles than for physical or worldly success. As he remarked in Act I, his elegances are spiritual, or moral, ones. De Guiche acknowledged this earlier in this act, when he admitted that with all his wealth and power, he was not as good nor as happy a man as Cyrano.

Rostand has managed this last act without any of the melodrama of Act IV. Cyrano's death is gentle, dignified, in character, logical, prepared for, and truly romantic. He does not really regret his life, and he dies with the satisfaction that the one recognition he wanted most — Roxane's — is his.

CHARACTER ANALYSES

CYRANO DE BERGERAC

Cyrano is, first and last, an idealist. He is not, however, a blind idealist. He does not expect tangible rewards for his idealistic behavior. When he throws his money to the players (Act I) he knows full well that he will be hungry, but the *beau geste* means more to him than material things — even food and drink. His own comfort never is a motive for action with Cyrano.

This idealist with his eyes open can also be a very intelligent man. He can disdain the very precise "establishment" rules because he does have such intelligence and competence. He can beat these people at their own game, though he does not often choose to play their game. For instance, Cyrano won the musicians for an evening because he had won a bet about grammar. At the time in which the play was set, grammar was a complicated and extremely technical subject. Cyrano knows all the rules for polite behavior and speech, but these do not matter to him as much as matters of the spirit.

Cyrano is as careless of personal danger as he is of personal comfort. He is truly a brave warrior. He remains calm and cheerful in the most trying of circumstances. He is such a good swordsman that he can fight off a hundred men. In battle he is brave, but he is also brave in the much more difficult situation presented by the siege. He never loses his courage, his good humor, his ability to cheer the other men. It is important to note that he is cool and collected when other brave soldiers become despondent. He is true to Roxane and Christian unto death. He never reveals that he wrote the letters which Roxane has accepted as coming from Christian. He always visits Roxane with delightful bits of gossip.

Cyrano never was successful in a worldly way. His play was never produced, though some of it was used by another. Even as a mature man he is often hungry, though he well knows that his talents could make him rich and famous if he chose to use them for that purpose. He is extremely versatile, and knows a great deal about many subjects. He simply does not ever choose to be rich or famous — he prefers to be right in his own eyes. He is inner-directed, in that the opinions and standards of the world really do not matter to him. He rebels by not playing the game;

he never adopts another's standards for his behavior; he is true to himself and his ideals.

This lack of change in the character could be a basis for criticism. Rostand has not created a growing, evolving personality. He did not try to do so. Cyrano was, at the beginning of the play, the epitome of the romantic idealist, and he remains so to the end. He is a perfect example of the type. The flaws of the character grow directly and logically from the perfection of the type. Cyrano is uncompromising, idealistic, faithful, brave, consistent, disdainful of acclaim and wealth, intelligent to the point of brilliance, creative, imaginative, witty, knowledgeable. Any change in the character would be a compromise of some sort. This is why Cyrano remains the perfect example of the romantic idealist—anything added to or subtracted from the character would make him less so.

ROXANE

The character of Roxane is difficult to accept at first. She is a romantic idealist, but seemingly not of the depth of character or intelligence of Cyrano. She is, rather, a *précieuse*. Her attention is on the surface of things, just as Cyrano's is on the roots. She seems as shallow as he is deep.

The character of Cyrano and that of Roxane offer many parallels. She, too, loves the *beau geste*. She goes to the battlefield with food, and to see her husband. She, too, is faithful until death. She, too, turns her back on the world, to retire to the convent to mourn her lost husband.

Cyrano and Roxane have many of the same ideals, though Roxane seems to see only the surface. She is attracted to Christian in the first place by his physical qualities, but she then attributes to him all the qualities that Cyrano has in such abundance, and she mourns Christian for these very qualities. When Cyrano dies and she learns the truth, she says that she has lost her love twice. One can only assume that she was blind to

Cyrano's true character because of her memory of Christian as she thought he was; she still sees Cyrano as the friend and companion of her childhood. Nevertheless her years of mourning are for the nobility of soul that she believed she had lost when Christian died, and not for the surface values of the *précieuse* she once was.

Both Roxane and Cyrano, then, are consistent, faithful, uncompromising characters, and both are dedicated to their ideals rather than worldly rewards. Both live in a dream world by choice.

DE GUICHE

In contrast to the two idealists, Roxane and Cyrano, we have De Guiche. He is a worldly, sophisticated cynic. He is motivated by personal desires rather than ideals. His own comfort means more to him than any noble idea. He takes revenge on Cyrano and Christian for having stolen Roxane from him by sending the regiment to almost certain death.

De Guiche would use anything at hand—power, influence, position, wealth—to get what he wants. He wanted Roxane because she was so beautiful; he would certainly not have married her with the idea of remaining forever faithful and devoted to her, even if he had not already had a wife. What he wanted was a rich and beautiful mistress.

De Guiche is the only character in the play who changes or develops, with the possible exception of Christian. In the last act De Guiche has mellowed considerably, to the extent that he has developed respect for both Roxane and Cyrano. He has learned to respect their spiritual values, though he does not completely share them, and he has learned that worldly rewards are not everything.

If Rostand had shown De Guiche undergoing a greater change than this, we would be very suspicious; if he had shown him not changed at all, we would be a little disappointed.

De Guiche is not able to adopt these ideals for himself, but he no longer is contemptuous of them in others.

De Guiche admits that Cyrano is probably a happier man than he is, though to all appearances De Guiche has everything a man could want. He is concerned about Cyrano and the threats to Cyrano's life: this is the same man who once sent Cyrano's entire regiment to what appeared to be certain death.

De Guiche has always had qualities of intelligence, wit and courage, but he lacked the nobility of character and dedication to ideals that Cyrano had. He is honest enough to admit that Cyrano may well have been right to choose the ideal, while realizing that the life of dedication to the ideal is not for him to embrace, himself.

In De Guiche, Rostand has treated a living, evolving human rather than a type. He is the villain of the piece, because he does try to win Roxane by devious means and because he does take his revenge. Yet he does not seek to evade the fire of battle himself, and he grows to admit that he was wrong, which takes some nobility of character.

If Rostand had given us a villain who was as purely villainous as Cyrano was a purely heroic hero, what a boring play it would be! The fact that De Guiche does develop and does show a brave spirit under fire contributes to the believability — if not to the realism — of the play. Also, with De Guiche's admission that his own views of life might be wrong, we have further subtle support in believing that Cyrano's views might be right.

CRITICAL COMMENTARY

CYRANO DE BERGERAC AS ROMANTICISM

Since *Cyrano* is so often referred to as a romantic play, a discussion of romantic and romanticism seems to be in order.

Three aspects of the words, "romantic" and "romance" should be considered by the student of *Cyrano:* romance, meaning a medieval, chivalric tale; romantic, as used in English literary criticism; and Romantic, as used in French literary criticism.

Romance, as a medieval tale, was a French literary form. During the middle ages, when the chivalric tradition was paramount in the minds of the upper classes, the chivalric tale developed. These tales concerned the daring deeds of the knights, and the relationship of the knights to their ladies. Many men were away from home during the crusades, and the tradition of the *chevalier servant* developed. This is particularly illustrated in *Roman de la Rose*, in which the *chevalier servant* loved his lady from afar. He wrote poetry, he served her in every way possible, but he never touched her.

The term "romantic" in English criticism most often refers to a treatment of a theme. Romantic treatments are sometimes sentimental, idealistic rather than realistic; Victorian literature is largely romantic, for example. The romantic attitude is quite different from the restrained neoclassical attitude. Reason, order, balance are earmarks of neoclassicism, while a wild, free exuberance is characteristic of romanticism.

French literary critics use the word "Romantic" to indicate the literary period from about 1827 to 1847. Hugo pioneered this period, and broke the rules of classicism forever. (See the section of this study guide entitled "Nineteenth-Century French Drama.") The freedom from the unities was exhilarating to the writers and audiences at the time. Vigny translated Shakespeare during the period, and Shakespeare became a hero of the Romantic movement in France. When critics said that *Cyrano* heralded a revival of the Romantic movement, or Romanticism, they were referring to a revival of this period. In actual fact, *Cyrano* was not a revival or a copy of the Romantic period plays; it is far superior to most of them.

Cyrano is a truly romantic play, harking back to the tales of chivalry; Cyrano is the perfect *chevalier servant*. This is a completely French play, a completely French hero. It is not at all like the romantic plays of Shakespeare, for example, and it follows few, if any, of the traditions of the French Romantic period. It is a spark of genius, growing out of French literary tradition, but not tied to any school.

NINETEENTH-CENTURY FRENCH DRAMA

During the Renaissance, France was slavishly following the classic patterns in its drama, particularly those laid down by Aristotle in his famous definition of tragedy. Plays observed the unities — of place (only one setting), time (twenty-four hours), and action (everything in the play points toward one major conflict). There was no violence on stage; battles and fights were told about, sometimes at great length. The plays concerned an important and heroic character, usually Roman or Greek, although one of the first French classic plays was *Le Cid,* by Corneille, which dealt with Spanish history. The heroes of these plays always had a tragic flaw and were dogged by fate. The plays were in verse. Racine, in the latter part of the seventeenth century, wrote such beautiful and perfect plays after this model that French drama of the eighteenth century was simply repetitious.

Romanticism was heralded in 1827, when Hugo published his "Preface" to *Cromwell.* He felt that although many of these classic plays were beautiful, they no longer expressed current tastes and needs in the theater and that there was a lack of development in the drama because of this slavish imitation. The first Romantic play to be performed in Paris was Hugo's *Hernani,* in 1830. Before the play was produced, he did all that he could to insure its success by reading it to his many friends. On opening night, the theater was full. Hugo had many supporters, and the classicists were also there in full force. Early in the play one of the characters drew his sword on stage, a breach of one of the cardinal rules of classic drama. The result of this defiance of the principles of the classic play was that a riot erupted in the theater, spreading rapidly to the streets of Paris. It was several hours before the gendarmes were able to subdue the warring classicists and romanticists. Later, this incident was to be called "The Battle of *Hernani*"; and it is interesting to note that the people who objected to showing violence on stage (among other things) were the ones who resorted to violence in the stalls of the theater.

The Romantics freed the French drama from the two unities of place and time. Hugo retained the unity of action, feeling that this was an artistic necessity. Local color was important in Romantic plays. The setting was more often Spain, though several plays were written about England and English historical characters, such as Cromwell and Mary, Queen of Scots. Violence was permitted on stage. The play often—indeed, usually—concerned a couple in love. Shakespeare was translated by Vigny during this period and became one of the idols of the French Romantics.

This new freedom in French drama was the beginning of much of the later development of drama in France and the world. Nineteenth-century France was not in a mood for much experimental drama, but the way was paved for the twentieth-century experimenters. The audiences in the nineteenth century in France were bourgeois, and they demanded entertainment of a rather light vein for their evenings at the theater. Consequently, with no intellectual (and wealthy) patrons to foot the bills for the playwrights, the theater became more commercial.

Some later developments in France in the latter part of the nineteenth century were naturalism and symbolism. Naturalism aimed at showing social conditions as they really were—usually as sordid as possible. Symbolists did not think that anything should be shown if it could be hinted at or symbolized. Closet drama, or static drama, was a development of this period. As little action as possible was shown on the stage, and the plays sometimes became very conversational.

Cyrano was written in 1897, and some people said that it marked a revival of Romanticism. It is a historical play. There is much local color in the various sets. There is action on the stage—

the sword fight in Act I is certainly violent, but it is also witty. It would be very difficult to imagine Cyrano without this display of his wit and courage and impromptu poetry. Very little else is shown, however, of violence. The fight with a hundred men is told about, as only the flamboyant Cyrano could tell it.

One of the earmarks of Romanticism is idealism. Certainly Cyrano is an idealistic person, and ideal takes precedence over common sense in his scheme of things.

Rostand never tried to imitate his success with *Cyrano*. Though there were other authors who did try to imitate it, it was not the revival of Romantic drama. It really did not belong to any school of drama which was current when it was written. Actually, if more of the truly Romantic plays had been of the quality of *Cyrano*, the period might have lasted longer.

Rostand does not seem to have been imitating the Romantics, though he used the freedom they had given to the French stage. He found an historical character who inspired him, an actor who could play the part, and the play resulted. While *Cyrano* is truly romantic in almost every sense of the word except that which denotes the French Romantic period, it does not fit into any school. It stands alone.

CYRANO AS A VIRTUOSO PLAY

Many critics have called *Cyrano* a virtuoso play, saying that it was written especially to capitalize upon the sundry talents of the famous French actor, Constant Coquelin. There is, of course, a precedent for thinking that Rostand wrote *Cyrano* with Coquelin in mind; he had previously written *La Samaritaine* specifically for Sarah Bernhardt. In addition, the dedication of the play, which reads, "It was to the soul of CYRANO that I intended to dedicate this poem. But since that soul has been reborn in you, COQUELIN, it is to you that I dedicate it," has also been pointed to as evidence that the play is a virtuoso play. If this dedication were written prior to production or publication of the play in the hope that such flattery would entice Coquelin to play the leading role, then it may well support this view. If, on the other hand, the dedication were written after production of the play, then it is more likely to be simply Rostand's way of thanking Coquelin for a job well done.

Another area which must be examined in any attempt to decide whether or not *Cyrano* was a virtuoso play is concerned with the main character of the play. In most, if not all, virtuoso plays the character is created to fit the abilities of the chosen actor. In *Cyrano*, Rostand did not create a character for Coquelin; indeed, he did not even distort the character of the historical Cyrano. If anything, the real Cyrano is less believable than Rostand's character. The only exaggeration of the character on stage is the size of his nose, and this is necessary in order that the audience may be able to see that the nose really is quite prodigious. One might object that the main character in *La Samaritaine* is a well-known character, Mary Magdalene. However, very little is known about Mary Magdalene, so Rostand was free to create a character to fit the unique capabilities of an actress such as Sarah Bernhardt.

Actually, *Cyrano* was probably the result of the happy conjunction of three things: the existence and availability of a virtuoso actor such as Coquelin, the re-discovery of the historical Cyrano, and the personality and ability of a playwright such as Rostand. As a man of the theater, Rostand was certainly acquainted with Coquelin and with the actor's great histrionic talent. That the playwright was interested in history is attested to by his choice of subjects for most of his other plays, and it is quite obvious that he was familiar with the recently discovered material dealing with his character's historical counterpart. And Rostand's own poetic and romantic nature might easily have created a desire in him to act as the catalytic agent which would bring the actor and the story together on the stage. In all probability, what happened was that Rostand's interests and personality made him want to write a play based upon the person whose exploits as a poet and soldier had just been brought to light. At the same time, luckily, he recognized in Coquelin the perfect actor to play the role.

Perhaps the final determination of whether or not *Cyrano* is a virtuoso play rests on the answer to one question: "Would Rostand have written *Cyrano* if there had been no Coquelin to play the part?" We shall never know the answer to that question. And that is unfortunate, because a playwright does not write a virtuoso play in the same way that he writes any other play. In a virtuoso play, the playwright includes bits of dialogue, action, even entire scenes for the sole reason that his chosen actor can do those particular things exceptionally well. And often these elements contribute nothing to characterization or plot. In reading *Cyrano*, the student might do well to examine it carefully and decide for himself whether or not the internal evidence indicates that Rostand inserted such elements.

THE PLAY AS HISTORY

During his lifetime, Edmond Rostand was in revolt against the important movements of his age—naturalism, symbolism, and Ibsenism—and all of his plays illustrated his idea that an illusion or unattained ideal is superior to real life. Although his plays, particularly *Cyrano de Bergerac*, are undeniably romantic, the Romantic movement in drama had been over for almost fifty years before Rostand wrote, and although anything as popular as *Cyrano* was naturally imitated, Rostand did not spark a general revival of Romantic drama. What he did do was to prove that historical drama was, and still is, a viable theme for the modern stage. Most of the characters and events in *Cyrano*—the conflict with Montfleury, for instance—are historical.

In *Cyrano*, Rostand had an opportunity to blend all his unique talents, interests, and spirit to produce a masterpiece; none of his other works, including the unfinished *La Dernière Nuit de Don Juan* (The Last Night of Don Juan), demonstrated his talents so well. In *Cyrano*, his southern spirit of exuberance, his lyricism, his fascination with unrequited love, all blended so well with the historical Cyrano's exploits that Rostand found in him the perfect subject. This seems almost to be a play of the seventeenth century rather than of the nineteenth century.

The historical Cyrano — Savinien Cyrano de Bergerac — was born near Paris on March 6, 1619. His parents, who were prominent but not noble, came from the town of Bergerac in southern France. And so, when he became old enough to care, Cyrano added "de Bergerac" to his name for the sole purpose of impressing people. He did, indeed, have an enormous nose, and on one occasion actually did describe it as preceding him by a quarter of an hour. In fact, he was such a renowned swordsman that no one else would have dared to make such a remark; many men died for much less. He entered the military profession, fighting and sustaining wounds at Arras. He retired because of his wounds and became a philosopher at the College de Beauvais in Paris.

The historical Cyrano wrote poetry, political pamphlets defending Mazarin, some plays — Molière really did use two scenes written by Cyrano — belles-lettres, and science fiction. His books on voyages to the moon and sun show his interest in science, and many of his ideas are startlingly modern. He was a Renaissance man — dashing, courageous, gallant, and intellectual. Like the Cyrano of the play, the real Cyrano was a man of many talents, high courage, and equally high spirit. He guarded his intellectual freedom and made many enemies, and he was destitute until he found a patron who suited him. Unlike the Cyrano of the play, however, he did find such a protector. And, like the Cyrano of the play, he was fatally wounded by a falling object — a stone, actually, instead of the log of wood mentioned in the play — which may have been dropped by an enemy. Some sources say that the accident, if it was one, happened in the house of his patron. He died on July 28, 1655. There is no record of such a romance as appears in the play, but Rostand has invented one which admirably suits the character and is dramatically necessary.

The real Cyrano, of course, was as much a man of his own time as Rostand was *not* a man of his own time, and perhaps that is what lends a note of authenticity to the drama. However foreign the ideas of Cyrano may be to any generation or country, they seem to strike a responsive chord in many and varied audiences. Cyrano is true to his own ideals and to himself, though he never really loses sight of reality or expects his quixotic behavior to be rewarded in any worldly way. He is true to himself merely for the sake of being true to himself—the ultimate idealism.

THEME AND IRONY IN *CYRANO DE BERGERAC*

Irony may be loosely defined as a distinct difference between what appears to be and what is. Since the main idea of *Cyrano de Bergerac* is the conflict between appearance and truth, it is obvious that theme and irony are closely woven in the play.

Irony is, of course, one of the most intriguing of literary devices. It has been in use at least since the early Greek dramatists, and it has seldom failed to capture the interest of an audience. And that is one of the major reasons that *Cyrano* has remained popular for so many years. Here are just a few of the ironies of the play:

It is ironic that Christian's beauty makes him appear to Roxane to be all that she thinks her heart desires, and it is ironic that Cyrano's ugly appearance hides from Roxane that which she truly desires—beauty of soul.

It is ironic that Roxane confesses to Cyrano, not her love for him, but for Christian. And it is doubly ironic when she begs Cyrano to protect the man she loves.

It is ironic that it is Cyrano's deception which makes possible the blossoming romance between Roxane and Christian. And it is even more ironic that when Christian tries to be honest, he fails hopelessly, and it is Cyrano's words and Cyrano's presence which enable Christian to marry Roxane.

It is ironic that Christian is killed before Roxane can be told what only Christian and Cyrano know — that the man she loves is, in reality, Cyrano. And this irony is compounded by the fact that it is Cyrano's letter which Roxane carries next to her heart, "like a holy reliquary," during her years of mourning.

The crowning irony — certainly, at least, for Cyrano — is that he is dying, not with "steel in my heart and laughter on my lips," but murdered by "a lackey, with a log of wood!" "How Fate loves a jest!" he says.

And, finally, there is irony in Roxane's discovery — too late — that it is Cyrano whom she has loved for so long. "I never loved but one man in my life, and I have lost him twice."

All these ironies and the many, many more that are to be found throughout the play add up to the great irony that appearance is not always truth, and truth is not always clothed in appropriate appearances. The eternal nature of this theme is one explanation for the continued success of the play. Another reason could be the suitability of the ending to the characters.

Imagine Cyrano as a husband. Imagine Roxane as a wife. Their romance, with Cyrano playing the part of the *chevalier servant,* could go on for all their lives; their marriage would have been miserable. But Cyrano did not really want to marry Roxane. She was lovely, and he loved her for exactly the same reasons that Roxane loved Christian. Christian is the only major character in the play who makes any attempt at being honest. He wants very much for Roxane to love him for himself. Neither Roxane nor Cyrano have any desire to face reality, however. They are happy in their make-believe world.

The historical Cyrano once killed a monkey. The monkey's owner, who operated a puppet show in Paris, had dressed the monkey as Cyrano, even down to a false nose. Cyrano heard of it, went to the puppet show and ran the monkey through with his sword. The owner sued, and Cyrano said that since the whole affair had taken place in the make-believe world of the theater, he would pay in kind. The judge accepted his payment—an ode eulogizing the monkey.

Just as the real Cyrano paid in the coin of the make-believe realm of the theater, so the emotions in the play are altogether theatrical—divorced from reality. The audience senses that this flamboyant character could never accept mere reality. He demands more from life. He fulfills the adolescent dream of an unrequited, tragic love. He is realistic enough to know that he could not have his cake and eat it too. He enters the pact with Christian with relish because it allows him to escape humdrum reality and to continue a delightfully boyish relationship. He is allowed to be misunderstood and tragic and to write beautiful love letters without the usual result of marriage and daily problems.

Just as *Huckleberry Finn* owes part of its charm to the return to childhood, so does *Cyrano*. These are children, not adults. Cyrano never faces adulthood, with its responsibilities, where he would not be able to toss his month's income away as a gesture. He would not want to pass up the *beau geste* because of duty. And Roxane enjoys her role as the grieving widow, solaced by visits from the attentive Cyrano.

In summary, *Cyrano* pleases audiences because it satisfies the adolescent dreams which are a part of all adults; it pleases because it is well-constructed and because the characters are consistent and romantic; and it pleases because there is harmony in the theme, characters, plot, and language. The ending is sad and bittersweet, but it is the only possible ending. It satisfies because any other solution to the ironic dilemma would be unromantic; a romantic play must have a romantic ending.

There is no jarring note in this play. The theme, plot, and characters are theatrical but somehow believable, because they are childhood dreams. The most fantastic thing about the play is that it is based on an historical character who was every inch as romantic and unrealistic and boyish and charming as the Cyrano in the play. The play has harmony and unity throughout, and allows us to live for a while in a make-believe world. The ending satisfies because any other solution to the ironic dilemma would be unthinkable.

STAGECRAFT OF ROSTAND

Cyrano de Bergerac could easily have been melodramatic if it were not for the fine balance of the play: the actions and settings are well-matched; the interest of the audience is held by color and excitement until the characters develop; and the costumes suit the setting, the mood, and the action.

Act I, in the theater, is lively and colorful. Act II is also in a public place, and many people appear on stage. The third act, on a darkened street, is very quiet. Cyrano's good deed—holding De Guiche's attention while Roxane and Christian are married— is performed in near darkness. Act IV again has the cadets on stage. The battlefield setting is not gay and cheerful, as are the first two settings, but it is still colorful. Act V is in the quiet courtyard of the convent. If Acts III and V were contiguous, the audience might well grow bored, but the color of Act IV provides contrast if not actual relief.

As interest in the characters develops, the settings have less intrinsic interest, and do not distract. The darkness of Act III is in keeping with Cyrano's dashed hopes and is necessary for the deception as well. And it is worth noting that, in Act V, most of the costumes—specifically, Roxane's mourning dress and the nuns' habits—are black, foreshadowing and complementing the idea of (Cyrano's) death.

REVIEW QUESTIONS AND ESSAY TOPICS

1. Point out ways in which Rostand shows Cyrano's personality, accomplishments, and character.

2. What is Rostand's attitude toward Roxane?

3. Is the appearance of De Guiche necessary in Act V? Why does Rostand include him in this act?

4. Discuss various ways in which Rostand prepares the audience for Cyrano's death and the resolution of his relationship with Roxane.

5. Does Cyrano have a "tragic flaw"? If so, what is it?

6. What purpose does Ragueneau have in the play?

7. In what ways does Rostand express the idea that the spiritual is nobler than the physical in life?

8. Is Cyrano's gesture of throwing away the bag of gold (Act I) characteristic of him? Is it symbolic? Does he do similar things elsewhere in the play? Discuss his character in the light of this gesture.

9. Discuss the ways in which each of these characters changes between his first appearance and his last in the play: De Guiche, Roxane, Ragueneau, Christian, Cyrano.

10. Discuss the dramatic contrasts in Act II.

11. Discuss Rostand's method of building suspense in Act I before the appearance of Cyrano.

12. Is Cyrano more tragic because of his nose? Considering Cyrano's nose, how does Rostand manage to keep Cyrano from being a comic character?

13. What can a reader learn about customs and society in seventeenth-century France by reading this play?

14. How does Rostand relate Cyrano's duel with the vicomte to the plot?

15. Is Cyrano a tragic or pathetic character?

16. Does Rostand make Cyrano a believable character?

17. Does the attitude of the cadets shed any light on Cyrano's personality?

18. Why does Rostand have Roxane marry Christian?

19. Point out Rostand's uses of irony in the play.

20. Why does Cyrano give Christian the letter in Act II and deceive Roxane?

21. Is Christian the antithesis of Cyrano? Is De Guiche? Is Ragueneau?

22. Where and how does Rostand use the dramatic device of comic relief in the play?

23. Do you think Cyrano's conduct toward Roxane was admirable or foolish? Why? Would Rostand agree with you? Why?

24. Is Rostand saying in this play that we should not overestimate the effect of our bad qualities, or put too much importance on them?

BIBLIOGRAPHY

There is a scarcity of book-length material in English dealing with either Edmond Rostand or his plays. The few books which have been written on the subject are no longer in print, but the student may be able to locate one or two such items if he has access to the library of a large university. The following is a list of several essays on Rostand and/or *Cyrano de Bergerac*, which appear in books more readily available.

BEERBOHM, SIR MAX. "Cyrano de Bergerac" and "Cyrano in English." *Around Theatres*. New York: Simon and Schuster, 1954.

BENNETT, ARNOLD. "Rostand." *Things That Have Interested Me.* New York: George H. Doran Co., 1921.

BERMEL, ALBERT (ed.). "Romantics: E. Rostand." *Genius of the French Theatre.* New York: New American Library, 1961.

CHANDLER, F. W. "Romanticists: Claudel, Richepin, Maeterlinck, Rostand." *Modern Continental Playwrights.* New York: Harper and Brothers, 1931.

CHESTERTON, G. K. "Rostand." *Five Types* (also, *Varied Types*). New York: Henry Holt and Company, 1911.

————. "Romance of Rostand." *Uses of Diversity.* London: Methuen and Co., 1920.

CHIARI, JOSEPH. "Edmond Rostand." *Contemporary French Theatre.* New York: The Macmillan Co., 1959.

CLARK, B. H. "Edmond Rostand." *Contemporary French Dramatists.* Cincinnati: Stewart and Kidd Co., 1915.

DUCLAUX, A. M. F. R. "Edmond Rostand." *Twentieth Century French Writers.* Freeport, N.Y.: Books for Libraries Press, 1966. (Reprint of 1919 edition.)

ELIOT, T. S. " 'Rhetoric' and Poetic Drama." (1919) *Selected Essays.* New York: Harcourt, Brace & World, 1950.

GOSSE, SIR EDMUND W. "Rostand's Plays." *More Books on the Table.* London: W. Heinemann Ltd., 1923.

HALE, EDWARD EVERETT, JR. "Rostand." *Dramatists of Today.* (6th ed., rev.) New York: Henry Holt and Company, 1911.

HAMILTON, CLAYTON MEEKER. "Edmond Rostand." *Conversations on Contemporary Drama.* New York: The Macmillan Co., 1924.

62

_____. "Edmond Rostand." *Seen on the Stage*. New York: Henry Holt and Company, 1920. (A different essay from the preceding.)

JAMES, HENRY. "Edmond Rostand." *The Scenic Art*. New Brunswick, N.J.: Rutgers University Press, 1948.

LAMM, MARTIN. "First Symbolists." *Modern Drama*. Tr. by Karin Elliott. New York: Philosophical Library, 1953.

MOSKOWITZ, SAMUEL. "Cyrano de Bergerac: Swordsman of Space." *Explorers of the Infinite*. Cleveland: World Publishing Co., 1963.

NATHAN, G. J. "Rostand." *The Magic Mirror*. New York: A. A. Knopf, 1960.

NICOLL, ALEX. "Neo-Romanticism in the Theatre." *World Drama*. London: Harrap, 1965.

PHELPS, WILLIAM LYON. "Edmond Rostand." *Essays on Modern Dramatists*. New York: The Macmillan Co., 1921.

_____. "Postscript: Rostand and France." *Twentieth Century Theatre*. New York: The Macmillan Co., 1918.

ROSENFELD, PAUL. "Edmond Rostand." *Men Seen*. New York: L. MacVeagh, The Dial Press, 1925.

SMITH, HUGH ALLISON. "Edmond Rostand." *Main Currents of Modern French Drama*. New York: Henry Holt and Company, 1925.

WALLEY, HAROLD R. "The Virtuoso Play." *The Book of the Play*. New York: Charles Scribner's Sons, 1950.

A few of the better editions of *Cyrano de Bergerac*, both in French and in English, available in this country in paperback are as follows:

The Leslie R. Méras edition of *Cyrano*, among the best available in French. It was published in 1936 by Harper Brothers, and is now in paperback.

Another French version edited by Oscar Kuhns and Henry Ward Church, published by Holt, Rinehart and Winston in 1960. Available hardbound or in paperback.

There are several translations available. One of the best is by Brian Hooker, in the Bantam paperback edition, and also in the Modern Library edition.

There are also several collections of plays which include *Cyrano:*

ROSTAND, EDMOND, and WILLIAM SHAKESPEARE. *Romeo and Juliet; Cyrano de Bergerac.* New York: Noble's Comparative Classics Series, 1965. (Revised edition). This is placed first in the list rather than in its proper alphabetical order because it may be of special interest, due to its specific aim of comparing the two plays.

GOLDSTONE, RICHARD H. (ed.). *Mentor Masterworks of Modern Drama: Five Plays. (Cyrano de Bergerac, Our Town, Pygmalion, The Crucible, Enemy of the People).* New York: New American Library, 1969.

POPKIN, HENRY. *Four Modern Plays, Series 2. (Rosmersholm, Cyrano de Bergerac, The Importance of Being Earnest, The Lower Depths).* New York: Holt, Rinehart and Winston.

WATSON, E. BRADLEE, and BENFIELD PRESSEY (eds.). *Contemporary Drama: Nine Plays. (The Hairy Ape, Street Scene, Abe Lincoln in Illinois, The Silver Cord, Justice, What Every Woman Knows, The Circle, RUR, Cyrano de Bergerac).* New York: Charles Scribner's Sons, 1941.

NOTES